To Missy

The Pearl of Great Price

God's Blessings Always!
Margaret Peterson

The Pearl of Great Price

Spiritual Poetry to Lift the Soul

by

Margaret Peterson

AuthorHouse™
1663 Liberty Drive, Suite 200
Bloomington, IN 47403
www.authorhouse.com
Phone: 1-800-839-8640

© 2008 Margaret Peterson. All rights reserved.

No part of this book may be reproduced, stored in a retrieval system, or transmitted by any means without the written permission of the author.

First published by AuthorHouse 4/7/2008

ISBN: 978-1-4343-3777-1 (sc)

Library of Congress Control Number: 2007908705

Printed in the United States of America
Bloomington, Indiana

This book is printed on acid-free paper.

Our mother, Margaret Peterson, has been devoted to her faith for as long as we can remember. We can't count the times she has reminded us to always ask God for guidance, to remember we are never alone, and to know He will never give us more than we can handle. She continues to inspire us by how she lives her life and we feel blessed to have her as our mother.

The Peterson Family

Acknowledgements

My heartfelt thanks to Jeanne and Peter Theberath and Kathy and John Tyler for their contributions in making this book possible, including the photographs, many of which came from the Tyler's own garden. The willingness of my entire family to help where needed on this project makes me very proud.

The photograph of the stained glass window is from the Church of St. Joseph, Rosemount, Minnesota, and is used with permission and gratitude.

God's Garden

Jesus, the gardener of my heart
Looked to see what had grown
Within the heart He had fashioned for love;
What kind of seeds had been sown?

He saw the weeds of envy there
For others' successes I'd seen
He saw a thorny and sickly plant,
A type of "I wish I had been."

Other weeds too numerous to mention
Choked out the plant that was me.
He said to Himself, "This all must be changed
But it will take time, I see."

He took my heart lovingly into His hands
And sweetened the earth with a kiss.
He gently removed my negative thoughts
And gave me a taste of His.

He told me He'd always be close as a thought.
I'd feel Him, at times, in a room.
On hearing these words, the flower that was me
Suddenly burst into bloom!

The Midnight of My Heart

When sadness comes or doubts assail me
Tearing me apart,
A darkness settles deep within…
It's midnight in my heart.

When family struggles weigh me down
Answers, I can't impart;
I know it's darkest before the dawn
But it's midnight in my heart.

Yet He who made the darkest night
Made the brightest dawn.
When I feel worst, I pray my best.
In God's time, cares are gone!

With deeper prayer comes deeper love
New thoughts of God can start…
Thoughts that all began when it
Was midnight in my heart.

How Deep to Pray

The deeper we pray, the deeper God listens,
For we must pray from the floor of our soul,
Always intent on praying with reverence
Wanting His will to make our life whole.

Then our prayer rises, like sweetest perfume;
Angels in Heaven notice it, too.
For God can bless the request we have made
Because He cares deeply if our dreams come true.

Dark Brilliance

Far beyond the farthest star
Where all is dark and still,
God exists, the same as here,
And He always will.

Summer

It comes just after springtime
With its crocus in the snow
Sweet bits of purple beauty
That makes us love them so.

Now earth becomes resplendent
With its brightly blooming flowers,
With their scintillating perfume
That enhances summer hours.

Sweet butterflies aflutter with
The very joy of living
Dance their way from flower to flower
While beauty, they are giving.

Could anybody not believe
That God is everywhere?
Tending each one as a garden,
Hearing every prayer.

Changes

I asked the Lord to make me strong
For I fall at the slightest touch.
He said, "I can't, my dear, because
You wouldn't need Me as much."

I asked the Lord to fill me with wisdom
"I want to be more!" I cried.
He said, "It wouldn't be good for you;
It's better if I guide."

I asked the Lord for untold wealth
To help the needy I found.
He said, "It's better to give of yourself
So love and joy can abound."

I asked the Lord how I could please Him?
Could I heal the sick and the lame?
He said, "It's not the great things you do
But all things in My name."

Life Without God

Life without God
Is a house so forlorn
That once held much laughter
And where children were born.

Where candles once burned
To celebrate an event
Like Christmas or birthdays
In great merriment!

Our souls are like this
If God doesn't reign
To guide us each moment
And heal us of pain.

We each must decide
With our sacred "free will,"
To choose God and His beauty
Or a house dark and still.

We're Not Alone!

In the darkness of life
When there is no light
To comfort and show us the way,
Close by each one
Is Christ, God's dear Son,
Ready to help when we pray.

Uncertainty

I sent a prayer of need to God.
It wasn't very grand,
More like a string, a tiny hope…
He held it in His hand.

More strings piled up. Did God care?
My hopes were growing dim.
He closed His hand and drew the strings
Around my heart to Him.

Where is God?

I see God in the mountains high,
I see Him very near
In people that I know and love
And hold so very dear.

I see Him in a starlit sky…
In every flower and tree.
I pray that when God looks my way,
He sees Himself in me.

The Hourglass of Time

Time is like an hourglass
Placed within our hand…
Precious as the air we breathe
Walking in God's land.

All the time we give to God
To use for good, untold,
Changes all our grains of sand
Into grains of gold.

My Lord

Unless You take my hand, dear Lord,
And show me where to go
My feet will stumble on life's path
And I'll be lost, I know.

But with Your help I'll do my best
To spend the time You give,
With every day reflecting You
Who taught me how to live.

My Guardian Angel

I have a Guardian Angel
That is mine, alone, to keep;
To guard me when I'm wide awake
Or when I'm fast asleep.

My angel has a mission,
To keep me Heaven-bound
And guard me from temptation
When evil lurks around.

I hope that up in Heaven
I'll see what I can't see,
My dearest angel whom I love
For all eternity.

God's Plan

Man was meant to sort things out
With help from his Creator.
The less he prays
The more trouble stays
'Till he kneels to Him sooner or later.

Our Unseen God

When trees are moving in the breeze
So gently to and fro,
It seems a sign that God is there
Letting people know…

We must believe that He exists
Though we can't see Him there
Watching over everyone,
Waiting for our prayer.

Portrait of Christ

In every soul there is a canvas
Waiting to be painted upon.
The brush strokes are our steps in life
From birth 'till time is gone.

We paint the living face of Christ
Day by passing day.
Strong and clear our strokes will be
If following Christ's way.

The things we do that aren't of Him
Cast a reddish stain…
For be assured, our wrongful deeds
Cause our Savior pain.

Golden deeds paint the halo
'Round our Savior's head
That once had thorns pressed in deep
Until our Savior bled.

Children, each a special child,
Paint with truth, not guile;
And loving words and loving deeds
Paint a little smile.

Nature's Love Song

In secret little wooded glens
Where no one ever walks
And only bird songs fill the air,
No one ever talks.

Nature sings wild hymns of love
In praise to God each day.
The Bible is unknown and yet
They follow Him their way.

Communion

I love to pray to God each day
To thank Him for my life
And know that I can turn to Him
To ease my pain and strife.

And when I take Communion,
That's the closest I can be
To God, the One with whom I hope
To spend eternity.

It's such a blessing we can know
His presence here on earth
Just like His twelve apostles did
Who came to know His worth.

When life is hard or when it's not
Still we need the union
That we can experience
When we receive Communion.

Dreams

A dream can occur by day or by night
A wish that can happen
But is not yet in sight.
Give yours to God who makes dreams come true.
For your dreams
Are His dreams
That He's dreaming too.

Peace

Clouds are drifting lazily
Across a sky of blue.
The sun is warming all the earth
With rays of golden hue.

Birds are singing melodies
Of love to God on high.
All is peaceful with my Guardian
Angel standing nigh.

Where is Eternity?

Eternity is all around us
Molding us to He
Who made each person for a purpose
And a destiny.

The Carpenters

Said Joseph to his Son one day,
"You must have a trade…
Do your best, then you will be
Proud of what you made."

Slowly, wisdom formed within;
How to measure wood,
How to cut and how to plane
And do the things He should.

Excellence came into view,
Pride in what He created.
Then came the day when Joseph and Jesus
And Mary all celebrated!

Their Son had become a carpenter now.
A respectable trade, for sure,
That filled their home with a sense of pride
And love that would always endure.

Character

The worth of a person
The inner being
Created by God,
All knowing, all seeing…

Molded and shaped
By day-to-day living,
Will we be selfish
Or generous and giving?

Those who ask guidance
From God every day,
Are deeply assured
They go the right way…

Onward and upward
To Heaven's golden gate.
Where God and His angels
View us and wait.

Point of View

Thank you for Your beauty, Lord.
At times I don't look out.
I only look within and see
My shades of pain and doubt.

But if I looked at You, Lord,
Amidst Your clouds on high
My worries would become as clouds
And softly drift on by.

We Work Together

"The Lord helps him who helps himself"
I learned but never knew
What its deepest meaning was;
Now I know it's true.

If our will is in tune with God's
Who rules all from the sky,
He quickly lends each one a hand
If we only try.

Fine Things

Once I said a prayer to God.
It was frivolous, I must confess…
That after He tended to all of the world
Was there room in His heart for a dress?

It had to reflect His excellent taste
So a bit of Heaven shone through…
Something that stood out from all of my things
And, to me, would always stay new.

I shopped at a store where the very first one
Caught my eye and my heart.
It was aqua; I felt it was made just for me!
God knew what was best from the start.

Opportunity

Along life's rocky road to God
We meet along the way
The One who wants to walk with us,
To each of us He'll say…

"Come, dear one, and rest a bit.
Put down that heavy load
Your cross that you've been carrying…
Great love for Me you've showed.

It's much too heavy for your back.
You need some help from Me.
I know how to carry a cross,
Plus, I'm good company!

Or…take your cross and walk alone.
Do what you want to do.
But you and I will both be lonely
All your whole life through."

When to Quit

When the cold winds of life
Blow steep in the soul
And bitterness reigns within,
It isn't time to give up on God
But for deeper prayers to begin.

Time

When God can seem to take too long
To hear our heartfelt prayer,
It doesn't mean He hasn't heard
Or simply doesn't care…

Rather, like the Bible says,
Take this as a sign;
The mill of God grinds very slow
But also very fine.

Dawn

When all the world is fast asleep,
The Lord of Love and Light
Spreads the dawn across the sky
And chases away the night.

No audience applauds the scene,
Though tickets should be bought.
Silently, He watches us
And hopes a heart will be caught.

Illusion

When night winds croon a lullaby
To stars that softly glow
Heaven seems much closer though
It really isn't so.

It still is where it used to be
All is in its place,
Waiting for the day when we
Can see God face-to-face.

Sunrise from My Window

We went to the window,
My angel and I
And watched God paint
The morning sky.

It started out softly,
Then took on a glow
That grew in brilliance…
A fiery show!

Oh God of all sunsets
And sunrises, too,
In all of this beauty
Let me see You!

The Time of Your Life

Each of us has a moment in time,
A bit of eternity
A tiny chance to live for the Lord
Sweet Savior of you and me.

But how will we fill each passing day
Before the hours have flown
Is there any way to ensure success
And cause a soul to have grown?

Asking God's guidance at the day's beginning
Shapes our own free will
To what the Lord has in mind for us
A job only we can fill.

The use of our time when guided by God
May still hold some moments of strife
But there is a joy in serving the Lord
It's called, "the time of your life!"

Salvation

A fallen person raised by the Lord
Is stronger than when they fell
For then His graces flood the soul…
A sweeter story to tell.

Mirrors

A mirror reflects
Whatever it views
We reflect
The paths we choose.

A Traveler's Prayer

Wherever I travel by land or by sea
I must have my God and my angel with me;
For all of the sites are more than just pleasure
I find that each place is a separate treasure…

With its own special beauty and people so dear,
My heart remains grateful year after year.
It's a gift to make friends in a faraway land
And happens because of the trip He has planned.

The grandeur of God can be seen everywhere
I must see as much as I can, for I care
About the whole world from the East to the West
With God and my angel, all journeys are blest.

The Great Unknown

Beyond the world of what we see
Is the life of spirituality!
The life of God within each soul
Inspiring us with every goal.

It rises and it courses through
Everything we think and do,
If we try to live His way
And take a little time to pray.

The Search

God is a prize that must be sought
No matter how busy we are.
He waits just as surely as Jesus Christ waited
While wise men followed His star.

For life would be wasted if never the soul
Could know its Creator, its Source.
As rivers flow back to the ocean of life,
Our souls feel God's magnetic force.

Once they are safe in His harbor of love
Talents bloom that were hidden before.
We fit into His plan, love our fellow man,
And are twice as alive as before.

My Happiness

When the sun is softly shining
And the sky is brightly blue,
Every breeze that dances by me
Seems to whisper, "I love you."

And it sets my soul to feeling
That my God is very near
So I thank Him for the life I have
And those I hold most dear.

Then I see the things worth having
Are the things that are for free.
Not fame nor earthly riches,
It's in God, my destiny!

Autumn Glory

When leaves once budded in the spring
Turn to burnished gold
Or scarlet red or russet brown
In splendor to behold…

It's then the world becomes for us
A magic place to stroll
Down winding little country lanes
That stir the very soul.

Could autumn be a hint of Heaven
With streets of shining gold
And colors even fairer still
Than ours so bright and bold?

Perhaps God gives us autumn days
To lift our thoughts to Him
Who has the best in store for us
By contrast, fall is dim.

God, the Artist

The Artist of the universe
Has never-ending ways
Of crowning nights with starry joy
And blessing all our days.

He uses colors rich and bold
But also soft and varied.
His autumn hues from distant views
Seem sweetly, gently married.

No spot on earth, however small,
Slips by His gaze, forgotten.
Bright skies of blue are dressed up, too,
With clouds that look like cotton.

He loves the dark lines that He draws;
He also loves the dim,
But mostly He just loves to draw
Our hearts and souls to Him.

The Bloom of Life

What can cause a person to bloom
To become a radiant being
Who moves about with confidence
And is worth the knowing and seeing…

Whose life is filled with purpose
With a sureness to each day?
The answer is God's saving grace
We obtain it when we pray.

And once the Divine is truly sought
A relationship can begin
That causes a soul to want to please God
And try to avoid all sin.

This is the very meaning of life!
A wondrous, uplifting sensation
That causes a person to value one's self
And adore the God of Creation.

Reflections

When I was just a little girl
My mother said to me
"Always say your prayers each day…
Come, say them at my knee."

I said my prayers so faithfully,
Worshipped Sundays, too.
Yet, God was always distant;
My mother never knew.

As I grew up, God still was distant.
Not 'til life turned bleak
Did I go running to the Lord,
A miracle to seek.

He gave me more than a miracle…
He walked into my heart
And healed the past that made me cry;
He gave me a new start.

Like stardust on a summer night
That sets a heart aglow.
The magic of His love is mine
Everywhere I go.

My mother's up in Heaven now
I wonder, can she see
My love for God that all began
With prayers said at her knee?

The Sign of the Cross

A breeze of grace brushed by my face
As I made the Sign of the Cross.
I felt a sudden closeness to Him
And appreciated His loss.

Lord, I want to reverence this sign
And never rush to be through,
Loving to spend the moment it takes
To show my respect for You.

Mary's Prayer

Dearest Jesus, sleeping sweetly,
How I love You, so completely!
You have come, God's chosen One,
To live on earth as my dear Son.

Did you hear the angels sing
Praising you, the newborn King?
We heard them in the stable here
And knew they sang for You, my Dear.

How could God have chosen me
From all the women that would be?
Did He see some specialness
You would find in my caress?

I am not unlike another
Yet am blest to be Your mother.
Forever will I thank God for
This little Son that I adore.

The Pearl of Great Price

God is the pearl
In the ocean of life;
Will we love Him or cast Him aside…
And spend our lives searching
For something unknown
To ease the longing inside?

Printed in the United States
124822LV00002B